BALANCING ACT

A Couple's Approach to Money

Brandon Smith

SDS Publishing

ISBN: 0692094598

ISBN-13: 978-0692094594

Table of Contents

Introduction

Everyone has a good idea what to do with their money. I'm sure everyone reading this knows not only what to do with the money they have now, but what they would do if they had even more. Of course there are the bills, the groceries, the gas for the car, and so on. There is also going above and beyond, like travel or college.

Being in a relationship is a great way to help advance those above and beyond items, as well as helping to share the load with everyday life. But what happens when we are in a relationship? The other person has their own idea of what to do with the money, of course. They will have their own spending habits. For half of those people out there, you probably think your partner spends too much. The other half will think their partner is too stingy. We can all agree that we don't want to argue or fight over money, but it happens often enough.

This book is dedicated to every couple that could not reach an agreement on their daily budget. There are many budget systems out there, but few if any consider the dynamics of the users who are trying to use them. There is one thing we can assume – that these two opposite personalities will be joined together to try to make the money system work.

This book explores the topic of how to make our money work with our dynamic relationships. We will apply some principles from various sources and introduce a household money system that is designed to enhance the relationships between ourselves, and between ourselves and our money.

The first half of this book will introduce and describe these principles. We will start by the fact that there are two basic personalities in a relationship – one that is sensitive, aware and structured, and the other that is free-flowing, spontaneous and unstructured. I believe that if a couple is reading this and I were to ask which one of them is uptight and sensitive about money, and which one of them is free-flowing and perhaps feels disengaged from the budget, they can point out who is who within a second. It's usually that obvious.

With the premise that both people need to be engaged in the daily budget process to make it successful, we will also find that both personalities are essential to a healthy budget and lifestyle. We need both personalities to be engaged and to be in agreement to making it work. Without these elements, the smartest budget program will fall flat on its face for the simple reason that slick tools are no replacement for a good working relationship.

But we don't need to throw slick tools overboard. In fact, the second half of this book introduces a money management tool that is designed to engage both parties and work for them. The important distinction here is that the tool works for us. We are not a couple trying to work for a tool.

With a healthy dose of understanding, we can find agreement and engagement over household budgets. Fights, misunderstandings and disagreements can be a thing of the past. I think you will agree with me that the budget that works for us is the budget that we all agree on and is easy to engage with.

Money Isn't Everything, But It Is Important

Our goal in this book is to develop and sustain productive relationships where it applies to personal finances. The concepts that will go into this effort will certainly apply to other areas of life, but the focus will largely be on the short-term control of money, and for a good reason: Many disagreements, misunderstandings and fights occur over money. And money is very important, whether we like that fact or not. If we can establish a productive relationship between ourselves and our money, then we'll have the keys to unlock productivity and enjoyment in other areas as well.

"Money isn't everything" is a popular saying. That is correct, but it is very important to recognize its importance and to learn how to control it.

Money is the tangible value that you earn when you exchange something for something else. For most of us, we exchange quite a lot of our time during the week for the money that we bring home. It is what we have to show for a long week's toil.

That we spent a long week at work earning this money, and that we were only given so much, it's only natural that how the money is used and allocated becomes a hot topic in the household. If we spent so much of our time trying to earn money, then why does it seem to run away from us?

I think you can agree with me that people spend an enormous time at work. We earn value for our employer and get a paycheck in response. Our society generally sets the baseline for this time commitment at 40 hours per week and many people easily exceed that number. With so much time spent in the service of an employer and in the pursuit of a single line of work, work and income become an identity. It in fact becomes the lion's share of one's identity after so many years and decades in this pursuit. If it is allowed to, it can displace everything else, such as relationships, marriage and kids.

This identity comes at the cost of tired nights, feeling worn out, exhaustion and frustration. I'm sure you can empathize. Coming home on the last night of a long week of work, only to have enough energy to collapse on the couch, or spending Sunday afternoon dreading work on Monday morning. Often, we feel that the good parts of life, such as friends and marriage and kids and fun hobbies, never get a fraction of their proper attention because our work takes up so much time and energy.

It is important to realize that the pursuit of money is a major portion of one's life and that emotions are consciously and subconsciously tied to this fact when we try to assess why our finances always seem to be running away from us. And when we don't agree with the use of money with the ones we are in a relationship with, it becomes a point of argument and discontent.

When the unfortunate argument erupts about how much money was spent where, we see that it can quickly strike at the center of someone's identity. As a result, it becomes a passionate topic. One person is bound to say something like "how is it fair that I spent so much time and effort, and indeed wrapped a good deal of my life around earning this money, only to have it fly out of our hands?" That person will feel all the worse if they believe the money was spent on frivolous things, or that it was spent and nobody can really say where it went.

The second person in the relationship will likely feel bad for making the first person upset, but they had their reasons for what they spent the money on. If they say they are sorry, chances are they are sorry about making the first person upset and think that saying sorry will patch things up. They want to avoid the conflict, move on and talk about something else more agreeable not because they feel guilty over the spending, but to avoid having an argument.

A typical response to these arguments is that "it's only money" and not worth fighting over. It is true that there are more important things than money and we should not fight over it. However, we can't simply ignore the energy and identity that went into that money in the first place. Invoking the phrase "it's only money" is a diversion to avoid the topic, for the honest reason that the person doesn't want an argument.

It is easy to illustrate other examples of relationship discontent over money. Imagine stumbling in through the front door after a long day at work. Your mind is tired and your body is hanging on its last thread. You are then presented with a bill that your significant other signed up for, over something you deep down don't really agree with, and is more than enough money to wreck the budget for the foreseeable future and prevent other things from happening that you were looking forward to. I congratulate you if you put on a good face in front of these circumstances, but it is very difficult to believe that your relationship will be anything but cool for the rest of the evening.

What happens to the relationship in this example? I think that many people would devolve into an argument at this point, likely with some heated statements driven from exhaustion and frustration. A skillful couple will be able to navigate it and still enjoy each other's company that evening, but this skill is rare. Perhaps the best that can be hoped for is a quiet and chilly night.

Here, an evening is wasted and goes nowhere for everybody. But life is short and evenings of cold relationships due to financial matters is not how we want to move forward. Besides, if our relationship only gets hot when we experience a financial windfall, it will not nearly be hot often enough.

Relationships Over Money

We cannot let money control the direction of our relationships. We must turn around the typical rut that we fall in where money defines how we treat each other. In fact, we must establish the fact that money does not lead to relationships. It is, in fact, the opposite: relationships lead to money.

This is a very important statement. The money we earn is derived from a relationship with other people. We create value of one kind or another for other people, and they reward us with money for that value. As we form good relationships, we have more opportunities for earning money.

Our relationship with our spouse or significant other has a financial dimension. In fact, it is one of the most important aspects of our financial future. Together, two people in a relationship can create more value together than if they were alone, and it is more than simply one plus one equals two. The collective energy of a relationship compounds and can easily lead to one plus one equals three, four, five, a hundred thousand or a million.

For example, a single person living alone must pay for everything themselves: rent, car payments, food, bills, gas for the car, and so on. In today's world, this can easily eat up everything that person is earning, leaving little for the future or even for opportunities to make a better future such as higher education.

Being alone, they have fewer contacts to lean on for financial help or guidance. Energy is needed to pursue a better financial situation, it is usually consumed with the immediate needs of life. Little energy or drive is left over for long-term change-making activities. Although they may have the desire to change out of their current circumstances, they are too deep in their current rut to get out. The financial world is unforgiving for those who are by themselves.

If you put two people together, the equation is much different. The basic bills from above are about the same with some increases here and there, but two incomes that are smartly managed may allow 20-30% of their earnings to go to extra purposes, which may range from date nights that invest in the relationship to higher education that invests in their job potential. Add on top of that mutual encouragement and teamwork, which are also essential ingredients. These investments create margin for truly great endeavors, such as pursuing college, having children, enjoying vacations and quality time together, obtaining a job of high responsibility and reward, or even starting a business.

However, two people who are at odds with each other can easily reduce their collective energy to zero as they cancel each other out. When this occurs, I can assure you there is disagreement--and perhaps even loathing--as both sides are frustrated that their collective efforts appear to yield nothing.

The issue here follows the old saying, "friends are like an elevator." They can take you up or they can take you down. Financially, being with someone can take you far higher than if you were by yourself, but it can also take you very low if it goes wrong. This leads us to the reason why this book exists – to enhance our relationships by making finances work for us.

The ideal state that we aim to achieve is a money system that works for our relationship and helps us to achieve our financial goals. As we wisely control our money as a team, we shall gain control over it. Money will not divide our relationship, but enhance it.

There are some people who may feel uncomfortable at the thought of money being used to enhance our relationships. This may be due to the thought that we should be able to love our significant other irrespective of finances, or as the wedding vow goes, "for rich or for poor." While I am not disputing this phrase, I will point out that money has a great purpose in helping us in our relationships. For me, one of the best uses of money that I can think of is investing in my marriage. I've never regretted the money spent on a date night or a couples-only vacation to Hawaii. On the contrary, it was perhaps the best use of money I've ever made and I'm happy to continue spending for those activities, as I'm sure everyone would be. To have money to do this makes it all the more important to have a budget system that ensures money is available for these valuable events.

Conclusion

In this chapter, we have laid down some important points that will carry us forward to financial success:

- Money is important because it represents a lot of our life's energy and effort.
- Good relationships lead to successful finances.
- Good relationships control money as a team.

In the next chapter, we will start to analyze how a couple's relationship typically works so that we can create a good working relationship with money.

Our Personalities

The first step in organizing a relationship-based budget system is to recognize how our personalities work. When we have a relationship with someone, whether it is a working relationship with a colleague or a romantic relationship, we often adapt our behavior in order to mesh with the other person. There are two general approaches that people take, and the best names to describe these personalities are "The Skin" and "The Skeleton"[1].

The Skin and the Skeleton is a relational concept that was developed by Pastor Ken Peters. After speaking about the concept in his church, he published a book on the concept: *The Skin and the Skeleton*. The idea is derived from generalizing the psychological with the physiological: each personality has behavior similar to those parts of the body.

---

[1] Peters.

The concept is nicely adaptable to our financial system and has the added benefit of not being tied to gender or background – we can have either personality acting within us despite our gender. The following is an overview of how this concept works.

The Skin and the Skeleton are two sets of behaviors that we may take on. We may often take one of these behaviors for one arena of our life and another for a different arena. Because the Skin and Skeleton are not tied to gender or situation, a woman can be a Skin when it comes to one arena of her life, like finances, and be a Skeleton in another arena, like working with children. Even more so, she can be a Skeleton when working with her own children but a Skin when working with someone else's children. The important part is to recognize which side you are currently acting on, and which side the other person is on as well.

The Skin

Our real skin has little in the way of structure, which introduces us to the Skin personality. The Skin personality is laid-back, flexible, avoids structure and flows with whatever it encounters. This makes for a resilient yet low-stress personality that can recognize new opportunities. The lack of structure allows the Skin to experiment, observe and be flexible.

Because it is relaxed and goes with the flow, the Skin personality doesn't really intend to hurt anyone's feelings and may bend quite a lot to avoid conflict. If the Skin is confronted with an issue, they will try to avoid conflict and either brush it off or avoid the issue. Responses like "it's no big deal" or "just roll with it" are common with the Skin.

If the Skin hurts someone's feelings, there is a good chance that it was unintentional and may even be unaware of what has happened. Because they believe they aren't looking to harm anyone, they may be unaware of the cases when they do hurt someone else's feelings. This is not to say that the Skin is oblivious, but it can appear that way.

The Skin avoids conflict. If the Skin is upset at someone, they tend to avoid the person and be passive-aggressive when avoidance can't be helped. A conflict means an issue needs to be sorted out between two people, and if the Skin seeks the easy way out, things may get worse in the long term. Sometimes conflict is good in that an issue will be confronted and solved sooner than later.

For example, if the Skin overspends at the store, they are probably not going to bring this fact up when they later meet up with their Skeleton counterpart because they think it will bring up bad feelings. The Skeleton is likely to find out later from other sources – probably because they watch the bank account more often. Why does this happen? The reason is that the Skin's personality is to go with the flow, avoid conflict and try to please everyone.

If the Skin does have a passive-aggressive streak, it may end up being self-defeating. For example, when a Skin is presented with a conflict, they may just say "blame me for it" as a way of quickly getting through this situation. Then they may resent doing just that – since they are Skin and generally subscribe to the saying "live and let live," they feel upset that they had to take the fall for something. From that point on, they may be passive-aggressive with the other person.

The Skin has many key traits that make it valuable. Flexibility is chief among them. If plans need to change, the Skin is quick to realize the change and move in a new direction. If the kids need some leeway (or perhaps mercy) with whatever they are doing, the Skin is likely to provide it. If dates and plans need to change, the Skin is likely to go along with it.

The Skin has to deal with a perception problem, however. The unstructured and flexible approach can be mistaken for disengagement and apathy. Observers may wonder "if this person changed direction on this issue so easily, then what do they really believe in?" This is a bit of an unfair criticism on the Skin, as Skins may hold deep-seated beliefs as all people do. It is a perception issue, however, and the Skin should be aware of it.

On the other hand, I suspect that few people have accused a Skin personality of continuing to bash their head against an issue that could have just as easily been bypassed. A Skin is valuable because they will recognize pitfalls for what they are and steer clear of them.

Summary of Skin Traits

Strengths

- Calm and collected demeanor.
- Willing to experiment and see what happens.
- Quicker to accept and adapt to change.
- Seeks to de-escalate.
- Able to navigate around obstacles.
- When faced with an insurmountable issue, will be more likely to bypass or circumvent than to expend resources by engaging it head-on.
- More likely to show mercy when mercy is needed.

Weaknesses

- The calm and collected demeanor may be perceived as being disengaged and maybe even apathetic.
- May let experiments and situations go too far before getting involved.
- May adapt to changes too quickly, or change and move in the new direction without much coordination with others.
- May take the easy way out to de-escalate, which may make things worse later on.

The Skeleton

The bones of our skeleton are highly structured and rigid, and this is a great name for this personality type. The Skeleton is a structured and rigid personality. Just like our bones, the Skeleton doesn't like to bend in ways it wasn't meant to. With the Skeleton, everything has its place and everything is done in the right way.

Plans are important to the Skeleton because they provide the structure required to get tasks done, whereas the Skin views plans as more of a guideline or a theme. If there is a project to be done, the Skeleton is going to pay attention to the structure of the group, the organization of the resources, and the details of the path to completion. There is a strong adherence to the plan.

The Skeleton's structure and rigidity comes with a very significant trait that defines a lot of its interactions with people: it is always on the look-out for potential issues. The Skeleton is quick to foresee problems, quick to seek to deal with such problems, and is less likely to yield.

The Skeleton guards its structure with a near-constant look-out for potential issues. High-level Skeletons will look for a hint or misperception which will cause a red danger sign to light up in their mind. For example, if a person is a Skeleton with finances and hears that their spouse is going to stop by the grocery store today after work, the Skeleton's mind is already anticipating the extra items that might end up coming home and fretting about the final cost.

Anticipating issues is a useful skill. However, the Skeleton might come across as untrusting, too sensitive, nosy or looking for a fight. This is not to say that anticipating issues and their solutions is a bad thing – quite far from it. It is an essential skill that when properly used can make life much easier. We are all familiar with problems that last too long and grow to be much greater than they had a right to be, if only someone had said something at the beginning.

As a result, the Skeleton is encouraged to develop one skill to counter-act this perception, and that is tact. Tact is the ability to address a future issue with another person while putting them at ease and getting their full involvement is a very valuable skill to develop.

Summary of Skeleton Traits

Strengths

- Thrives on structure and organization.
- Sensitive to developing situations.
- Eager to resolve issues.
- Will not bend to issues and will be resolute when strength is needed to overcome.

Weaknesses

- May be perceived as being too structured and unyielding.
- Perceived as seeking and creating conflict, even though the Skeleton's real purpose is to resolve the conflict.
- May be perceived as too sensitive or nosy.

How it Works

After reviewing the two personalities, it is important to remember that they are not tied to gender or background. A single person can be a Skin when it comes to one thing and a Skeleton when it comes to another. It may often depend with whom we are working with. In those cases, there is usually some way that our personalities decide which stance we will take.

For example, if you are working with a co-worker on a project and find that they are a definite Skeleton, you may find yourself being a Skin in response. As they get more structured and tackle issues head on, you might find yourself responding by going with the flow and finding flexibility and compromise. But if you work on the same kind of project with someone else and take a definite Skeleton approach to it, the other person may respond by being a Skin. It is often situational, but the important part is that you recognize who is taking which role so you can work with them effectively and appreciate the value the different personality brings to the table.

I'll offer myself as an example. In the family finances, I am the Skeleton. I watch the financial ledger almost daily and keep a running tally of income, expenses, bills and so on in my head and can recite it on demand. It's not that I want to – it just seems to be my nature to pay attention to it. My ears are always sensitive to any hint of a coming bill or expenditure. I can tell at about what moment during the day that my wife is walking into the store, and my mind is already calculating what the damage will be.

But when it comes to our kids, I am the Skin and my wife is the Skeleton. My wife's kid-radar is always up and sensing. She is quick to respond to any noise from across the house that sounds like strife, hurt feelings or hurt body parts. I, on the other hand, am a Skin on this topic and I keep a much looser rein on the kids. I am more inclined to let them figure their own issues out, and when things get too far, more inclined to challenge them to find their own solution. My happiness comes when I see the kids figuring out their own situations.

Both Are Right

In this example with the kids, who is more correct as a parent? The answer is both, so long as both are present. The kids need someone to watch them closely and to discipline them when things get out of line, but they also need space to learn, space to dig into a situation over their head and space to try thinking for themselves about how to fix the situation. So long as the Skeleton and the Skin are present, I believe the correct answer is "both."

The important part here is that neither side is right or wrong when they are combined with their counterpart. My wife and I do well with the kids when we are working as a team: the kids get space to experiment and learn, combined with discipline and structure. It's easy to tell when the balance is off, such as when my wife is gone and has left me with the kids. I have to adjust my personality to add more structure to my Skin in order to keep the house from being burnt down;

it is easy to tell that I'm slightly out of my element when the Skeleton is gone.

The same principle applies to our money. It is right that one person is watching the ledger closely, tracking expenses and making sure the finances stay afloat and get the attention that is due them. It is also right that the Skin demonstrates how to relax from such a stressful topic and advocates for the use of money in ways that makes life more enjoyable. Either personality alone is unbalanced – the Skeleton is prone to stressing out and the Skin is prone to not being careful. But by putting them together and operating in harmony with each other, the best of both worlds is combined. Easier said than done. Let's look at how to get this system to work.

Defining Success

It is easy to draw an illustration of how a Skin and Skeleton may interact over the budget. When two people come together with common finances, the Skeleton personality is usually the one to pick up the job of money-watcher. They will watch the bank account, track expenses, and make plans for how the money is to be used. With their radar up and sensing, they are aware of most every transaction that clears the bank. They may enjoy the colorful pie charts and bar graphs of watching their money. Thus said, the Skeleton may also instigate a lot of arguments--usually starting with the classic phrase "You spent how much on that?"

What then does a successful middle ground look like? How can we combine the Skin and the Skeleton to work in harmony for our finances?

This chapter will define what success looks like when we combine a Skin and Skeleton over the topic of finances. The picture of success described below is just a guide. I encourage you to modify and create your own picture of success to suit you.

Remember, neither side is wrong, but each person brings a different aspect to the table that needs to be addressed. Both parties should give input and find agreement on several points that, when combined, will create a holistic win for your personal finances.

What We Want

The Skeleton believes the finance system is successful when:

- The budgets are being maintained and they almost always end in the black.
- They feel confident that the Skin is actively participating with honest intentions.
- They have intelligent short-range and long-range financial plans that are working.
- There appears to be no problematic issues on the horizon.

The Skin feels that the finance system is successful when:

- They have an easy and simple interaction with the finance system. It is not distracting or convoluted. It is fast, easy and shows them only what they need to know in a few short seconds.
- They believe their spending is balanced and responsible.
- They feel their voice is heard in the financial decisions. They are not shut out of the process.
- They believe those items that they believe to be important are getting funded, including the "over and above" ones.

- They agree the financial process is easy to engage with and is not confrontational.
- They feel arguments over finances are minimal.

The criteria listed above represents a good middle ground. The Skeleton gets to do what they do best – make plans and put them into action while being assured that issues are being handled. They believe that money is going to worthwhile items and that every day is a step toward achieving their larger goals. They appreciate hard data that shows this progress, such as spreadsheets, graphs and bank account alerts.

The Skin, whose attention on this topic may be hard to get, will enjoy a simple easy-to-see interface that shows them only what they need to know. The Skin isn't blinded by charts, long spreadsheets or other busy products that shake off their attention. The successful system for the Skin is the one that gets their engagement, and part of that is won by being uncomplicated and easy to use. It will resemble more of a touch point that shows them the information that just pertains to them and sets a lower bar for participation than it does the Skeleton.

As we can see, the same tool will not work for both personalities. To build a system that achieves our objectives, some other concepts need to be pulled in that will tie our objectives together and make them effective and repeatable.

One of these concepts is a regular time cycle, which will help to make the budget system repeatable and easier to sustain. Once the system becomes a simple habit on a recurring schedule, it becomes easier to sustain for the long term.

Another concept that we'll use to build our financial powerhouse is a visual management system. This kind of system filters down information from various sources, which our Skeleton is most familiar with, and condenses it down to an easy format that shows the Skin just what they need. A simple system allows everyone to participate with the plan in a way that best suits them. For example, after a long day and getting home late and exhausted from work, nobody cares to have to update their financial situation on a special system that requires time and energy to interact with – especially if the alternative is as easy as checking a box and moving on.

The next chapter will delve into how to develop such a financial system.

Building the System

Setting the Pace

Pace and rhythm are important to managing personal finances. The rhythm of life is apparent, especially if you are one of the many people whose rhythm includes waking up early, going to work, coming home, eating dinner, and so on. Organizations also seek a rhythm, and indeed one popular method is to set up a rhythm to a team's pace and set a structure around it. This principle is called a sprint, and we are going to take this as a tool for managing our finances.

The concept of a sprint is simple – it is a period of time that sets the pace for work. The task is sized to fit inside that time frame.

For a software team, tasks and issues are sorted before the sprint begins. Some are put into the sprint's planned workload while others are deferred for later. When the sprint begins, the team begins on the workload that was planned for that sprint. When the sprint ends, the team can see how they did. If they got all of their tasks done early, hooray for them – they finished ahead of time, management can be happy, and the team can work on catching up on other things or pulling in future work until the sprint period is done. If, however, the team didn't get everything done, that is okay – all of the unfinished work is combined with the backlog of work and hopefully everyone is a bit wiser for what can be accomplished given the work and time. The planning team for the next sprint goes through the backlog and selects the items for the next sprint, or maybe other issues that have risen in priority take their place instead.

While this system establishes a nice rhythm for working on tasks, it also provides an amount of forecasting that allows the group to have a very good sense of their rate of progress. This allows them to tell their management how fast they will get things done with a good degree of certainty.

Circling back to personal budgets, we need a time base that makes for a nice rhythm. Usually, this is set by how often your paychecks arrive. Many people receive their paychecks every two weeks, and this usually turns out to be a good sprint period. It is neither too long nor too short. You will usually have a good idea of what you'll be doing in the next two weeks to be able to forecast what you'll be spending your money on.

In the two week sprint, the next sprint starts when the next paycheck arrives. Just before it arrives, you can plan for what will happen in the next two weeks and allocate money for it. This includes how many times you might fill the gas tank in your car, how often you will go to the grocery store, and any special events or activities you will be doing that will require some money. Parents of children will be sure to put up the expense of a date night if they are lucky enough to get one during the upcoming sprint.

The sprint starts on its assigned day. As the days progress, you can simply and easily update the sprint's plan on the visual management board. Planned expenses are ticked off as they happen. Unplanned spending gets noted on a little ledger. In my experience, unplanned expenses always occur. The important thing at this point is to capture it so you at least have awareness of it as the sprint progresses.

As the sprint comes to its close, you can see how well the plan worked out and if the budget will end in the red or the black. In all of the sprints I've done with my family finances, I can't ever recall one going exactly as planned or the final balance being an even $0 at the end. Things change at the last moment, something turns out to be more expensive than originally thought, and so on. Putting together a rigid plan of expenses for an upcoming sprint is a strong temptation on the part of the Skeleton personality, and when things don't go according to plan, the Skeleton is sure to be disappointed and possibly upset. What causes things to go against the plan--and what to do when the plan falls apart--is a topic unto itself that we'll cover in a later chapter.

The sprint example above was for a two week period, but everyone is able to choose the period that works best for them. For example, if your paycheck arrives monthly, you of course are free to choose a monthly sprint. However, it's probably asking a bit much to have a really good plan of what expenses will look like for an entire month. At the beginning of a month, it may be hard to forecast all of your expenses for the month, because you may have only a hazy idea of what you'll be up to three or four weeks from now. If your paycheck arrives on a monthly basis, it would be a good idea to split the month in half and reserve half of the paycheck for the second half of the month.

If you aren't able to do a two-week sprint, you are certainly free to find a time period that will work for your sprints. A week is as short as you'll want to go – you'll probably have a very accurate view of planned expenses with just a week ahead of you. Anything less may get tedious to plan, although some personalities might work well with a daily sprint.

Another scenario arises if your income is not regular, or comes out of multiple sources that aren't coordinated. The important thing to keep in mind is to pick a period of time where you have a good estimate of what income will come in during that time, and what your expenses will be during that period.

To review the sprint duration, you want to pick a regular period of time where you are able to reasonably forecast:

- Your upcoming expenses, and
- Your income.

If the period is too long, your ability to forecast gets hazy and becomes vulnerable to overlooked items or surprises. If the period is too short, the process of organizing, launching and reviewing sprints may be a burden.

Visual Tool

Now that we are going to use sprints for putting a rhythm to our personal finances, we need some tools to manage the sprints. How do we satisfy the Skeleton's highly tuned sensitivity to the finances and the Skin's happy-go-lucky spending?

We need a system that combines these two personalities. The Skeleton needs data and scrutiny. They need a viable plan that holds water and accounts for every detail. We also need something visual and simple for the Skin, else they will view it as a burden and put it off. Remember, our goal is to create something that allows both personalities to participate in the finances and to be able to tell the money what it will be doing for them.

We need a piece of visual management. This tool is found plastered all over the walls of companies that use lean methods. They consist of pictures, charts, graphs, lines and so on, describing all sorts of key metrics that deserve scrutiny by the team. The goal of these materials is that for whatever they describe, they are to be simple, visual, easy to understand and posted where everyone can see them.

It is just this kind of tool that our Skin needs to help them uphold their part of the finances. This tool is designed to be easy to understand and easy to interact with. As we discussed before, the Skin goes with the flow and anything more complicated will cause them to opt out and pass it by. Our tool, or at least the public-facing part of it, is therefore tailored to the Skin's daily use.

Here, we put away the eye-crossing ledgers and tedious data entry. A one-page tool that can be printed and posted on the refrigerator is the goal. This page very quickly allows both the Skeleton and Skin to see the status of the finances, and just as importantly, provide a very quick and easy way of listing the expenses. The easier it is to interact with, the more likely the Skin will be willing to use it on a regular basis. If we can win the Skin's daily participation with managing finances, then we have won a major victory.

The rest of this chapter uses images from a spreadsheet example. The original spreadsheet can be downloaded from www.balancing-act.life. I encourage you to visit the site and get a copy of the spreadsheet. It is free to download and since it is in a popular format, you can personalize it to your own needs.

The sprint page gets posted in the house right as the sprint starts. A popular place is on the refrigerator with a magnet, but any place will do so long as it is visible and the Skin won't forget about it.

The page has three sections. The first section represents the planned expenses for the sprint, each with a check box. When each sprint is planned, expenses can be forecasted. It is impossible to forecast everything, but usually when two people can sit and think about it for a moment, they can assemble a good picture of what is coming. They can tell about how many trips to the gas station and grocery store will occur. They know of special events coming up that need money. They know how many times the kids will need lunch money. As items are added in and tallied up, we can select which items will fit in the sprint and which ones will have to be deferred for later.

When we get to "rack and stack" our budget requests, we can agree together which ones need to be done in the upcoming sprint, and which ones can wait. Here we have won another victory – we are now telling our money what it will be doing.

Each item that is selected for the sprint has its estimate listed as well and goes next to a checkbox. As those expenses are completed, we simply check the box. The sample form has a couple boxes already checked as an example. As those planned expenses are taken, they are simply checked off. You filled up your gas tank on the way home? Easy – find the line for one tank of gas and tick the box. Done! You are now free to continue with your busy day and you've hardly spent three seconds updating your finances.

TWO WEEK PLANNER	Sept 15 Sept 28		FORECASTER	Sept 29 Oct 12
PLANNED EXPENSES:			Wish List	Cost
x	Date Night + Babysitter	$100	FENCE PARTS	$50
	Museum Trip	$40	CAR OIL CHANGE	$40
	Kids Lunch Money	$20	DATE NIGHT	$75
	Wife Hair Cut	$40	BOAT MAINTENANCE	$250
x	Week 1 Groceries	$200		
	Week 2 Groceries	$200	Kids Birthday	$50
x	Gas	$32	New Dishes	$75
	Gas	$32	New Couch	$400
	Gas	$32		
	EXTRA:	$50		

The section below the planner is for unplanned expenses. Based on my experience, it is best to have a sum of money available for unplanned expenses because they always happen. Here, unplanned expenses can be listed and a running tally kept of how those are adding up. If you put aside an amount of money to cover these, you can see how this amount is being consumed.

The unplanned expense ledger is also a space to trade money. Maybe something important came up at the last minute. One option is to check off a planned expense and move its amount into the unplanned section to take care of the last-minute item.

This section is probably the most challenging for the Skin. Recall that the Skin wants to get along and not cause controversy, and they are probably aware that writing down an unplanned expense is sure to register on the Skeleton's radar as soon as the ink has dried. Since Skins avoid conflict, they may avoid conflict by not listing unplanned expenses at all – or in other words, not participating anymore. Here, the Skeleton needs to be patient and encourage the Skin to participate. Here is a good rule for the Skeleton: do not get upset about unplanned expenses so long as they were listed. Honesty won't be penalized.

As the sprint goes by, the bottom of the unplanned ledger usually turns up to a tally of how well the sprint performed. Ideally every budget ends in the black, but in my experience that is not always the case. When – not if, but when – the budget ends with a negative sign at the bottom, the key is to not get upset. Instead, go back through the ledger and figure out what happened, and apply the lesson to future sprints. Is someone always getting coffee at work, which probably equals $5 per day for 10 working days in a sprint? That will certainly add up. Next time, add it to the planned expenses. Not only will your coffee spending be recognized, but you can relax about not having to hide the expense from your significant other because it was agreed upon already – so long as you check the box when it has been spent.

In fact, one noticeable effect of the sprint is that the items identified in the planned section are actually encouraged to be made. Since your item has been planned, now is your chance to make it happen.

Forecasting

Up until now, we've talked about how to create and manage a household budget that is workable and effective for everyone. At this point, we hope the Skin is engaged and the Skeleton is feeling understood and in control. As sprints go by, even though they may not all end up perfectly, hopefully at least agreement and understanding have been reached and that arguments triggered by money are rare, if not gone entirely.

As we use this budget system, we will become aware of how much money is spent on things that are important in the short-term, but we haven't yet seen how contribute to the long-term vision. This leads us to one of the most important objectives: forecasting.

One of the most powerful things we can do as Personal Finance Managers is to tell our money what it will do for us. Too often we have outsiders telling us what we should do with our money: the bank, cable company, utilities, and cell phone companies all have expectations on the money we earned, and are equipped with systems such as automatic payment options to ensure that our money does what **they** want it to do. But who makes sure that we have money to spend on what we want? The bank is not going to help fund a vacation or a fun birthday party for the kids. Can your personal initiatives get the same firm commitment as what the bank gets?

For this result, this budget process includes a page for forecasting. It is your opportunity to anticipate future spending and plan for it. The process is simple – just sketch in what the item is and an estimate of what it will cost.

The Forecaster section should be available for anyone to list what they think they should spend money on. It is a chance to brainstorm and dream about the future. It doesn't matter if the item is small or large – it is just as valid to list a cheap men's hair cut as you would list a Hawaiian vacation. As such, this is usually the Skin's favorite section.

Here, we position the list right in front of the Skin and encourage them to pencil in ideas whenever they can.

The important part here is that the Skeleton should not dismiss or make caustic remarks about the items the Skin wrote down. As we discussed above, the Skin and Skeleton each bring something valuable to the relationship. Those valuable things will be different, yet meaningful and irreplaceable in their own way. The Skeleton may often struggle to appreciate the things the Skin may put on the forecaster, but here, understanding is very important.

Whatever you do, don't erase lines without mutual agreement between the two of you. If you don't agree with something on the list, keep the item written down until you've talked it over and understand why the other person added an item. Our system is designed to open communication with one another and work together as a team.

My advice for the Skeleton:

- No negative remarks! You don't want to chase the Skin away from the process.
- Remember your timing. Would the Skin's seemingly frivolous item actually work with the budget at some other point in time? This is not a license to indefinitely postpone Skin's items, but perhaps some negotiation with price and time will yield a good middle ground.
- If something expensive and important is coming up, you can always set up a monthly "payment plan" on the budget.

My advice for the Skin is to:

- Stay engaged and list items as you think of them. Think along these lines: If you write down what you want, then you are that much closer to getting it!
- Don't let a lack of exact figures stop you. If you have a notional activity but don't know how much it would cost, list it anyway. Your Skeleton may be able to help you with the details – let them help!
- You may not get all that you want, but if you have items on the list, you'll be able to sort out what can come sooner or later.

Negotiating the Planned Budget

So far, I've described the planning process in broad terms, where budget items are created and put on the planning table. However, this process deserves more attention, as it can cause quite a bit of contention.

Almost every budget will have more requests than money to cover them, which can make money a bit scarce. The entire planning process needs cooperation and understanding to make it through to an agreeable solution.

Looking deeper into the planning process, we pull together two pieces of information – what items need money for the upcoming sprint, and how much money is available. The latter is a bit easier to determine, and the next chapter will address how that amount is determined. For now, imagine all of the bills have already been covered in the budget – this means the rent/mortgage, utility bills, and so on. We are left with the amount of money left over from the bills that can go to the more fungible items in our lives – groceries and gasoline being the most common, but also frivolous things like date nights, saving for vacations, or the mundane necessities like saving up for new car tires.

When this "left over" amount of money is known, we can start filling in the planning sheet with the known items from the Forecaster list. Each planned item deducts from the spending total, so we can get an idea of how much we have left.

Both the Skin and Skeleton should meet together to assemble this list in person as each person will have valuable input from different viewpoints. It will help if the forecasting sheet has already been filled in because it is easier to simply bump items from the forecast side to the planned side. As you go through several sprints, the rhythm of selecting planned items becomes easier.

Planning a budget cycle is an exercise in compromise. Nobody will get everything they desire or wish, but everyone should agree that the budget is fair to all.

Detailed Planning

When the budget planning cycle was described, the Skeleton probably noticed that not all of the budget items were being discussed. Where were the utility bills, rent/mortgage, car payments and so on?

The reason these items are set aside is to provide focus on discretionary spending, whether it be food or gasoline or date nights. To bring the entire budget into play during a budget cycle planning session will make it more complicated and may chase the Skin away.

There is a budget process that is under the hood, so to speak. It deals with the known and fixed bills, such as utilities, mortgage/rent, and so on. Usually this is the domain of the Skeleton, since they are more inclined to deal with financial details. Skins are welcome to run this system too, although it's usually enough to ask that they understand what it does and that it is handling what it is supposed to. Let's look at what's under the hood of our budget process so both the Skin and the Skeleton are on the same page. Remember, understanding is the key our system here. We now add the Monthly Budget Planning and Sprint Worksheet.

The Monthly Budget Planner tool is easy to use. The monthly budget items are entered in and their costs are estimated. Most items will have fixed costs that are well known, such as mortgage/rent, memberships, subscriptions and car payments. Others are an estimate, such as water and electricity bills. However, usually these can be estimated with a good amount of accuracy.

Monthly Budget Planner

Current Month	OCTOBER		
Typical Bills	Forecast	Actual	Difference
Cell Phone Bill	$70.00	$70.00	$0.00
Internet Bill	$34.99	$34.99	$0.00
Gym Membership	$40.00		$0.00
Car Loan	$321.55	$321.55	$0.00
Home Mortgage	$1,300.00	$1,300.00	$0.00
Kids College Savings	$100.00	$100.00	$0.00
Car Insurance (Monthly)	$205.00		$0.00
Water & Garbage Utility	$150.00	$148.57	$1.43
Electric Utility	$60.00	$61.22	-$1.22
SUM	$2,281.54	$2,281.33	$0.21

In the table shown above, estimates are shown in the "forecast" column and actual amounts are shown in the "actual" column as they are actually paid. The sum of the forecast column is used to calculate the monthly bills and feeds into the Sprint Worksheet.

As bills are paid, their amounts can be entered into the actual column. The far right column indicates the difference between the forecast and actual columns and provides a running total of how accurate the estimate was.

The table shows example bills that have already been paid and ones that are still waiting to be billed. If the month ends and there is a blank space, then it's good to find out why. Did a bill get lost? Or did it go away – or are we ever that lucky?

The table also shows examples of slightly variable bills such as electric and water bills. Since they will be slightly different than the estimate, then the Delta column will show the combined effect. A black number means we came out ahead, while a red number means we paid more than anticipated.

It is important to get together every couple of months and review the entire budget to see if it is appropriate and to ask questions. Can certain bills could be reduced or eliminated? Is there is room in the budget for a car loan? Can the vacation fund be increased?

The next tool to introduce is the Sprint Worksheet.

Sprint Worksheet

Income:	$2,450	← 1.	Enter income for the period.
		← 2.	Adjust for excess/loss from previous period here. Loss is
Carry-Overs:	$0		entered as negative.
Bill Payer:	$1,141		
Savings Desired:	**$150**	← 3.	Savings desired for this period.
Post Bill Budget:	$1,159		
Planned Expenses:	$1,109		
Post-Planned Total:	$50		

The Sprint Worksheet is updated for every budget cycle and ties everything together. Because it has to be checked every budget cycle, it is supposed to be as easy as possible to understand and update. The gray parts are automatically calculated, while the black parts require your interaction.

The income for the sprint – whether planned or actual, depending on your income situation – is entered at the top as Step 1.

Step 2 allows you to adjust the income. Say your last budget came in over-budget by $63. You have the option here to enter -$63 here to balance out your previous budget by taking from the upcoming budget. Likewise, if you didn't spend everything in the last budget, that amount can be applied to the next budget by entering a positive number. Step 2 allows us to make these adjustments without having to dip into savings in order to cover a shortfall from the last budget.

Step 3 is important: savings. Often overlooked, this is important because it allows you to pay yourself. It could go into the Monthly Budget Planner, but usually there is a balancing act between managing the planned budget items and the amount going into savings. Kudos if your savings amount is consistent and locked-in every month, but many people may find that they need to flex savings against immediate spending. For whatever your situation, that amount is entered here.

The rest of the table is automatically calculated. It works as follows:

- Bill Payer: This is the total of the Forecast column from the Monthly Budget Planner, divided by the number of budget sprints in the month. This allows you to spread out your monthly bills over the monthly income. Beware that this may mean you need to have extra cash on hand at the start of the cycle to cover immediate bills before your income arrives.
- Post Bill Budget: The amount of money you have for discretionary spending. It will be this amount that you negotiate with for the planned budget items.
- Planned Expenses: This is the total of the amount you allocated for planned budget items.
- Post-Planned Total: This is the money left over after everything has been allocated. It shows up on the ledger portion of the visual management tool as the "extra" amount for unplanned expenses.

It is designed to be simple and easy to use in the long term. On nights when the budget needs to be reviewed and you don't have the energy to concentrate on it after a long week at work, it helps to have a simple and lightweight system that works.

This system does not address more advanced topics such as retirement planning or debt reduction. There are many resources available for these that offer great strategies, and this tool can certainly help in implementing those initiatives on a consistent basis.

Bringing It All Together

For an example run-through of this budget system, we start by taking a look at how the current budget cycle is ending. The first step is most important – get together with our significant other. This is a budget for couples. Despite the temptation to knock it out individually, we both need to participate.

The first question that is usually asked is "how did we do?" Was the budget plan roughly on target? Or did a bunch of unexpected things happen? A typical budget will have a mixture of both. A precautionary note: The Skeleton needs to be patient and understanding and not chase away the Skin. Instead, everyone must apply their lessons for next time.

The next step is to check the Sprint Worksheet and go through Steps 1 through 3. Steps 1 and 2 are usually well known and quickly entered. The ability to set an amount for savings in Step 3 gives you a meaningful and reachable goal to reach for later in the planning process.

The final step is to put together the visual tool. We can dig in by checking the Forecast ledger and see what items are due to be bumped into the planned section. Next, we can think about the upcoming weeks ahead and estimate what is going to be spent. If you are using the spreadsheet, it will update our amount left over as we enter planned items. Hopefully we can avoid having to adjust savings in order to fit in all of the planned items. If we do have to balance savings and the planned budget, we can at least read the planned items list and know what is causing us to go over it again.

Once the planned section is lined out, the process is finished by printing out the visual sheet and attaching it somewhere accessible. As the budget kicks off, we can quickly check off planned items as they occur, or write in unplanned items as they come up.

Again, I encourage you to get a copy of the spreadsheet that was shown in the previous chapters at www.balancing-act.life. The download is free and you can personalize your own copy.

Final Thoughts

We are all different through our personalities, upbringing, financial experience and relationship situations. This system is not rigidly outlined and is meant to be adapted to your particular situation. I encourage you to modify this system to fit your needs.

As a final note, remember that the goal of all of this is to have a financial system that leaves our relationship at the center and in control. Success is defined by how well we negotiate together and agree on how our money works for us. Money is often a spiritual reflector – we use and perceive it as a mirror of ourselves, and as discussed in the beginning of the book, that is for a good reason: a lot of who we are went into earning our money.

We can all be blessed if we achieve relationship happiness and wealth at the same time, and I hope this financial system can help achieve that for you.

How This System Was Developed

As with many things in life, this system grew out of several seeds that were planted over a long period.

The first seed was as early as late 2003 and early 2004 when Pastor Ken Peters developed the Skin and the Skeleton paradigm. At that time, he was speaking in detail about the topic and proposing a future book about the subject. I had recently graduated from college and married my high school sweetheart. We were members of his church in Spokane at the time and thought that the Skin and the Skeleton was a profound idea. The concept helped to explain so much of how we as newlyweds were responding to each other. In some topics I was behaving like a Skeleton – rigid, organized and sensitive to disturbances – while my wife was behaving like the Skin – going with

the flow, seeking to please and avoiding conflict. Depending on the
topic, our roles would reverse.

I began to see this paradigm play out at my workplace as well.
Depending on what stance my co-workers seemed to subconsciously
take, I would take the opposite role. In the presence of a Skeleton, I
would turn into a Skin, and so on.

My wife and I moved so I could take an electronics engineer position
in the Seattle area. As I moved through engineering circles in the area,
I was exposed to the "Agile" and "Lean" workplaces – two major
trains of thought that often collide in a technology and manufacturing
company. At those places, I was exposed to these two methodologies
and to a myriad number of ways on how to actually implement them
and live them out. Some methods seemed to work and provide great
value, while others seemed to be more work than what they paid back.

By 2011, we had a two-year old daughter and another daughter
coming soon. My wife had quit her job to be at home with the kids and
to incubate her own business in her spare time. In addition to being an
electronics engineer, I had also joined the Air National Guard, where I
did the one weekend a month and couple weeks a year routine for a
local engineering squadron. During 2011, I was "voluntold" to deploy
to Afghanistan for over half a year. This adventure took up most all of
2012.

One thing about a deployment is that you might have long periods of
time with not a lot to do. Such is the soldier's life. But the nice thing
about modern war is that it is very easy to video-chat back to home.
One thing my wife and I tried to do was to pick up a household
budgeting workbook that was popular at the time and study it
ourselves to take advantage of the financial boost the deployment

offered. We would then use Skype to try to talk it through and implement it.

For those not familiar with a military deployment, for all of the hassle and interruption it causes, I give credit to the Pentagon for making it worth my while. Pay in a combat zone is tax free and there are several allowances that are added in as well. Money is often like water and we didn't want this deployment money to slip through our fingers.

I recall the financial workbook being an excellent application of graphs, tables and numbers. It all made sense to me, the engineer. I could also tell that my wife was not connecting with it. I couldn't blame her – she was essentially a single parent with a three-year-old kid and a seven-month-old baby on her hands. And as per my advice, she was using money to get things done. She hired a landscaper to take care of the lawn, anything mechanical that I would have fixed or maintained myself was instead sent to a shop, and so on. Being a financial Skin, she used money to make things work and didn't want to fuss about it.

When I arrived home, I chucked the financial workbook into the garbage. Did I think it had the advice inside to make proper use of our finances? Yes. But did I think our mix of personalities could make it work successfully? Nope. We needed a system that worked **for** us and **with** our mix of personalities.

With that in mind, in early 2013, I hammered out the elements to the system described in this book. I took my wife's Skin-like approach to the subject and tried to give her exposure to just what she needed to know. I came up with a simple check-off sheet and planner that allowed us to bite off our finances a few weeks at a time. It was essentially a Skin and Skeleton-oriented approach that used some Lean and Agile concepts to give it a structure and rhythm.

We kept up with this system from early 2013 and we continue to use it. With almost five years of this system under our belts, I can definitely say it helps. Does every budget end in the black? No. Frankly most go over a little bit. We've learned to set aside a typical amount to cover the usual overages that occur. Do I stand by every other Friday to punch out a new spreadsheet and post it on the refrigerator to launch the next sprint? Well, usually a couple days into the sprint we have it ready to go (Sunday night, usually). We are human, which means we procrastinate, deviate from plans, and experience unexpected needs.

As we've developed this system, we've learned to get each other's input in the planning stage, which helps both of us feel better that the budget is addressing each of our needs. I've learned to accept what my wife spends without complaint so long as she lists it on the tracker and stays involved with the system. As mentioned above, there is no penalty for being honest.

Over the years, visitors to our house would see the budget paper on the refrigerator and ask about it. After we explained a bit about the system, they thought it was a great idea. When I explained the personality differences between us and how this system tried to work with both of us, 100% of our visitors responded that they felt the same way. I was then nudged to bring this system to a larger audience, which resulted in this book.

I thank you for trying this system and hope that your relationships and your finances can find real benefit from this system.

Notes

1. Ken Peters, *The Skin and the Skeleton*. Audio tapes from Covenant Faith Center, Spokane, WA, 2004. Also available in book form from Open Heart Ministries, 2007.

Made in the USA
Middletown, DE
04 June 2018